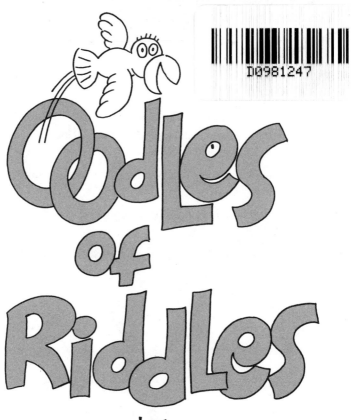

Oodles
of
Riddles

by
LORI MILLER FOX
Pictures by Sanford Hoffman

 Sterling Publishing Co., Inc.   New York

Library of Congress Cataloging-in-Publication Data

Fox, Lori Miller.
  Oodles of riddles / by Lori Miller Fox ; pictures by Sandy
Hoffman.
      p.   cm.
  Summary: A collection of riddles on such topics as TV, monsters,
aliens, and shopping.
  Includes index.
  1. Riddles, Juvenile. [1. Riddles.] I. Hoffman, Sanford, ill.
II. Title.
PN6371.5.F69   1989
818'.5402—dc19   89-4549
                                                                CIP
                                                                AC

10   9   8   7   6   5

Published in 1990 by Sterling Publishing Company, Inc.
387 Park Avenue South, New York, N.Y. 10016
© 1989 by Lori Miller Fox
Distributed in Canada by Sterling Publishing
% Canadian Manda Group, P.O. Box 920, Station U
Toronto, Ontario, Canada M8Z 5P9
Distributed in Great Britain and Europe by Cassell PLC
Villiers House, 41/47 Strand, London WC2N 5JE, England
Distributed in Australia by Capricorn Ltd.
P.O. Box 665, Lane Cove, NSW 2066
Manufactured in the United States of America

Sterling ISBN 0-8069-6880-X Trade
            0-8069-7202-5 Paper
            0-8069-6881-8 Library

CONTENTS

1.	Show Stoppers	5
2.	Haunted Howls	13
3.	Animal Crackups	19
4.	Home Silly Home	25
5.	Crazy Eats	29
6.	Good Sports	35
7.	Shop To It!	39
8.	Mad Months and Jolidays	43
9.	Water Water Everywhere	47
10.	Bored of Education	53
11.	Funidentified Flying Objects	58
12.	Outrageous Outdoors	61
13.	Crime and Pun-ishment	65
14.	Happily Ever Laughter	71
15.	Drive Yourself Crazy!	75
16.	Party Lines	81
17.	Funny Business	87
	Index	93

*To my mother, from whom
I inherited my sense of humor*

• 1 •
SHOW STOPPERS

What monster hangs around talk shows?
The Phantom of the Oprah.

Where do talk show hosts go for sun and fun?
To the Geraldo Riviera.

What does a maple tree like to watch on TV?
Sap operas.

What do horses do for entertainment?
Watch Stable TV.

How is a smashed TV set like a retired surgeon?
Neither one operates anymore.

FUN AND GAME SHOWS

What's a wild cat's favorite TV show?
"Leopardy."

What's a gunfighter's favorite TV show?
"Win, Lose or Draw."

What's a dolphin's favorite TV show?
"Whale of Fortune."

What's Danny Devito's favorite cookie?
Shortbread.

What famous puppet ate curds and whey?
Little Miss Muppet.

What do disc jockeys surf on?
Radio waves.

What is grey, wrinkled and sings songs?
Babar Streisand.

Who gives you a haircut, a shave and a song?
Barber Streisand.

What singing chipmunk designs jeans?
Alvin Klein.

What spaghetti sings opera?
Pasta primadonna.

What brand of fruit punch do sopranos drink?
Hi C.

What do you say when you want a horse to sing an encore?

"Mare! Mare!"

What does Fred Flintstone sing while he drives?

Car tunes.

CARTOON COMICS

What cartoon character lives in Jellystone Park and eats health food?

Yogurt Bear.

What does Boo Boo Bear drink?

Yogi Beer.

What do you call a cartoon about Humphrey Bogart in Jellystone Park?

Bogi Bear.

What did Humphrey Bogart say to the fish at the piano?

"Play it again, Salmon."

What is a cowboy's favorite movie?
"Lasso Come Home."

Who is the tallest Jedi?
Luke Skyscraper.

In which Star Wars movie did Darth Vader play a referee?
"The Umpire Strikes Back."

What did the glamorous ape wear to the Hollywood opening?
A monk stole.

Why was the actor's hair always messy?
Because he never had a good part.

What is a musician's favorite cereal?
Flute Loops.

What musical instrument does a crabby Scot play?
The nagpipes.

What chord is the hardest to play on a guitar?
A telephone cord.

What's a weatherman's favorite musical instrument?
A foghorn.

Why won't weathermen tell each other jokes?
They don't want to laugh up a storm.

What deodorant does a popular musician use?

Rock and roll-on.

MUSICAL CHEERS

What's a bee's favorite musical?
"Stinging in the Rain."

What is a millionaire's favorite musical?
"Guys and Doll-ars."

What is a fish's favorite musical?
"Coral Line."

What is a dog's favorite musical?
"The Hound (Sound) of Music."

Why did the soda bottle take music lessons?
It wanted to be a band liter.

What did the band leader say to the barber?
"Take it from the top."

Why did the outfielder join the orchestra?
So he could play first bass.

What do you call a ballerina when she's late?
  Leotard-y.

What did the ballerina buy at the hardware store?
  A tutu-by-four.

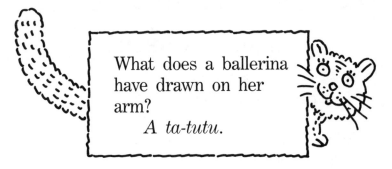

What does a ballerina have drawn on her arm?
  A ta-tutu.

How do native American ballerinas dance?
  On their teepee toes.

Where do bad jokes serve time?
  In the pun-itentiary.

How do comics like their eggs cooked?
  Funny-side-up.

What is a hockey player's favorite brand of comedy?
  Slapstick.

Why did the whale leave show business?
  It wanted to get out of the spoutlight.

• 2 •

HAUNTED
HOWLS

Who turns into a tired animal at every full moon?

A wearywolf (werewolf).

What is invisible, weighs 2,000 pounds and eats peanuts?

An ele-phantom.

Why did Casper the Friendly Ghost always ride up in the elevator?

He wanted to lift his spirits.

Why do so many monsters become great photographers?

Because they love being in dark rooms.

What did Frankenstein climb to get to his room?

Mon-stairs.

What is the first thing Frankenstein reads in the daily paper?

The horror-scopes.

Who does Frankenstein take to the movies?

His ghoulfriend.

What do you call it when a warlock thinks about his girlfriend?

Witchful (wishful) thinking.

What do witch doctors say when they get married?

"I voodoo."

What do wizards serve tea in?

Cups and sorcerers.

What did King Kong wear to church?

His Sunday beast (best).

What do you get when King Kong slips on a glacier?

Crushed ice.

What happens when King Kong steps on a piano?

It goes flat.

What does Big Foot ride to school?
A bicycle-built-for-toes.

Where does a ghost look up words?
In a diction-eerie.

How is a regular dictionary different from a witch dictionary?
In one you learn how to spell words. In the other you learn how to word spells.

What did the mixed-up witch eat for breakfast?
Scrambled hex.

What do witches' Rice Krispies say?
"Snap, cackle, pop!"

What's the largest spell?
A jumbo mumbo.

WITCH IS THE FAVORITE?

What's a witch's favorite game?
Hide-and-shriek.

What's a witch's favorite dance?
The hocus-polka.

What's a witch's favorite bird?
The sea ghoul.

What's a witch's favorite Beatles song?
"The Ghoul on a Hill."

What's a witch's favorite song?
"What Kind of Ghoul Am I?"

What do witches put on their front doors?
Warlocks.

What do warlocks sell at art fairs?
Witchcrafts.

Where do witches sail?
Off the Pacific ghost.

What do you hear when a witch breaks the sound barrier?
A sonic broom (boom).

What does Count Dracula drink to stay awake at night?
Cups of coffin.

Why was Igor the Hunchback so embarrassed?
Because he made a ghoul of himself.

How did Igor know which horse would win the race?
He didn't—he just had a hunch.

What did the genie say at the laundromat?
"I'll grant you three washes."

What do you say when you are attacked by mythical dwarf-like creatures?
"Sticks and stones may break my bones, but gnomes will never hurt me."

• 3 •

ANIMAL CRACKUPS

Where did Dumbo the Flying Elephant land?
At the earport.

What does an elephant do when it's frightened?
It ele-faints.

Where do Australians play with their wild animals?
In kanga-rooms.

Where do kangaroos look up words?
   In pocket dictionaries.

Who would steal from kangaroos?
   Pickpockets.

What does a moose do when it's stuck in traffic?
   Honk its horns.

What famous little deer lives in the town of Bedrock?
   Bam Bambi.

What does a brontosaurus do when it sleeps?
   Dino-snores.

BEARLY FUNNY

What kind of letter does a bear send a lion?
Wild ani-mail.

What kind of bears like to bask in the sunshine?
Solar bears.

What do polar bears use for paste?
I-glue.

What does a Japanese polar bear wear?
An Eskimo-no.

What does a bear use to part her hair?
A honeycomb.

What do giraffes do when they fall in love?
Neck.

What do you throw at jungle animals when they get married?
Wild rice.

When do rabbits fly to Niagara Falls?
When they're on their bunnymoon.

WHAT DO CATS PURR-FUR?

What's a cat's favorite side dish at lunch?
Mice-aroni.

What's a cat's favorite side dish at dinner?
Mice pilaf.

What's a cat's favorite dessert?
Mice cream.

What's a cat's favorite drink?
Miced tea.

What cat eats grass?
A lawn meow-er.

What sound does a turkey judge make?
"Gavel, gavel!"

What do turkeys say when they don't make sense?
"Gobble-dy-gook."

Who is the richest animal in the world?
A mule-ionaire.

DOGGONE IT!

What is the snootiest dog?
A cocky spaniel.

Where do you look for a missing dog?
At the lost and hound pound.

Where do you buy fresh dog biscuits?
At a barkery.

What do you get when you cross a black dog and a white dog?
A greyhound.

What do performing dogs do after the show?
Take a bow-wow.

What does a duck say when it's in a rush?
"Quick, quick!"

What does a rooster do with a pencil and paper?
Cock-a-doodles.

Who tells us how horses vote?
A Gallop poll.

What do sheep wear
to keep their hooves
warm?
Muttons.

What state has the most cows?
Moo Jersey.

Where can you read up about famous cows?
In "Moo's Who."

• 4 •

HOME SILLY HOME

Where do wealthy painters live?
On easel (easy) street.

Where do they keep the Goodyear Blimp?
In a high-rise building.

What did one entryway think of the other entryway?
That it was a-door-able.

Why did the door get fired?
It was lying down on the knob.

Where does a seal hang pictures?
On the living room walrus.

How do you hang up an idea?
Inside a frame of mind.

How did the American Indian unlock his door?
With a Chero-key.

Where can you find the finest basements?
On the best-cellar list.

How can you tell if your porch is bored?
See if it's awning (yawning).

What does a window do when it's cold?
Shutters (shudders).

Where did the table donate money?
To a chair-ity.

How does a chair put on pants?
One leg at a time.

How does an American Indian cover the hole in his pants?
With an A-patch-e (Apache).

What do lizards put on their bathroom walls?
 Rep-tiles.

What do you take when you have a phone in
the bathroom?
 Babble baths.

What illness did the chimney get?
 The flue (flu).

What piece of furniture will never learn to
swim?
 The sink.

What stove stands alone and wears a mask?
 The Lone Range.

Where do Siamese twins sleep?
In double beds.

What did the couch say when asked how it was feeling?
"Sofa (so far), so good."

What do bricklayers clutter their homes with?
Brick-a-brac.

What happens when knicknacks get scratched?
They become nicked-nacks.

What does a sheep put over a light bulb?
A lamb shade.

What was the name of the mixed-up electric company?
Con Fused.

• 5 •
CRAZY EATS

Who delivers breakfast, lunch and dinner, and always completes his appointed rounds?
The mealman.

What do Californians eat for breakfast during a tremor?
Earth-Quaker Oats.

What cereal goes, "Snap, crackle, squeak?"
Mice Krispies.

What do chess players eat for breakfast?
Pawncakes.

What does a wacky chef use to get the wrinkles out of pancakes?
A waffle iron.

What do you get when you cross a pig and a wildcat?
Sausage lynx.

Where do swimmers sit to eat lunch?
At pool tables.

What do millionaire first-graders eat for lunch?
Peanut butter and jewelry sandwiches.

What do millionaires put butter on?
Bankrolls.

What do X's and O's put butter on?
Tick-tack-toast.

What does Smokey the Bear spread on his toast?
Forest preserves.

What does a slice of toast wear to bed?
Jam-mies.

What do you get when you mix Snoopy and Sunday brunch?
A beagle and cream cheese.

What cheese can't stop talking?
Chatter (cheddar) cheese.

What computer comes with lettuce, tomatoes and special sauce?
A Big MacIntosh.

What is Sigmund Freud's favorite after-school snack?
Milk and kookies.

How do scarecrows drink milk shakes?
Through straws.

What do worms chew?
Wiggley Spearmint Gum.

Who holds the title for the noisiest chewing?
The world chomp-ion.

What is the noisiest food in Italy?
Spaghetti and meatbells.

What brand of spaghetti sauce does a baby eat?
Ragoo goo.

What is a baby's favorite Chinese dish?
Goo goo gai pan.

What do silly chefs cook?
Beef, stew-pid (stupid).

What does the Lone Ranger serve with meatloaf?
Masked potatoes.

What do foot doctors eat with their hamburgers?
Bunion rings.

Who does Clark Kent turn into when he's hungry?
Supperman.

What happens to pasta when it laughs too much?
It gets spa-giddy.

What is a bullfighter's favorite pasta?
Ravi-olé!

What is a knight's favorite dessert?
Pie à la moat.

How do you eat evergreen ice cream?
From pine cones.

What ice cream treat jumped off the Empire State Building?
A banana splat.

How does a gingerbread man close his raincoat?
With gingersnaps.

How does the Pillsbury Doughboy file his cookbooks?
According to the Doughy Decimal System.

What does the Pillsbury Doughboy drink when he's thirsty?
Baking soda.

What does a mean kid get when he eats too much?
A bullyache.

What old-west cowboy always belches?
Wyatt Burp.

Why was the wacky chef laughing?
Because he cracked a good yolk.

Did the wacky chef kiss the food goodbye?
No, but he micro-waved.

• 6 •

GOOD SPORTS

What athlete can do everything?
  A jock-of-all-trades.

What does a brontosaurus get when he works out too much?
  Dino-sore.

Where do small town body-builders hang out?
  In hunky-tonks.

What are a prizefighter's favorite colors?
Black and blue.

Who is the world's most patient person?
The heavywait champion.

Who is the most popular person at a fist fight?
The belle of the brawl.

Who is the most violent umpire?
A rougheree.

When do pigs score in baseball?
When the last little piggy runs wee-wee-wee all the way home.

What do catchers eat off of?
Home plate.

What did Babe Ruth do when his car wouldn't start?
He walked home.

What president can hit a home run and split logs?
Babe Lincoln.

When train engineers and farmers get together, what sport do they take part in?
Track and field.

JOCK JOKES

What is a con man's favorite sport?
Racket ball.

What is a carpet's favorite sport?
Rug-by.

What is a plumber's favorite sport?
Toilet bowl-ing.

How do you win money bowling?
You strike it rich.

When do jockeys control the weather?
When they hold onto the rains.

Why did the golfer need a new club?
Because he had a hole in one.

What do you get when you hit a quarter into a toll booth with your golf club?
A toll-in-one.

What do you get when you cross a card game with a golf game?
An ace in the hole.

What does Arnold Palmer drink on a cold day?
Iced tee.

How do sheep cheer for their football team?
"Sis! Boom! Baa! Baa!"

What is Gladys Knight's favorite cheer?
"Pip! Pip! Hurray!"

Why didn't the football player finish school?
Because he was left-back.

When do football players tell jokes?
At laugh time (half time).

• 7 •

SHOP TO IT!

What do you call the celebration of 200 years of shopping?
The buy-centennial.

How would you describe a boring, ordinary shopping center?
Run-of-the-mall.

What is the heaviest kind of chain?
A chain of stores.

Where do you buy laundry detergent?
In a soapermarket.

Where do you buy knee-highs?
In the sock (stock) market.

Where do flowers shop?
At Blooming-dales.

What is a clothing salesperson's favorite game?
Tag of war.

Where does a store keep its extra clothes?
In a wearhouse (warehouse).

What clothes have too much starch?
Hardwear.

CONSUMER HUMOR

What kind of telephones do imposters buy?

Phoneys.

What kind of parasols do dummies buy?

Dumbrellas.

What kind of timepieces do liars buy?
False alarm clocks.

What kind of stockings do firefighters buy?

Pantyhoses.

Where are good products manufactured?
At a satis-factory.

What lemon buys things at auctions?
The highest bitter.

What mall sells only knives?
A chopping center.

In what shopping center do you meet famous people?
The Mall of Fame.

How did the Wright brothers find out about the clearance sale?
They got a flyer.

What is the strangest kind of commercial?
An oddvertisement.

What happens to business when pants sales are slow?
It slacks off.

When are dress shops impossible to get into?
When they're clothesed.

What kind of stores do sailors shop in?
Boat-iques.

What kind of stores do ghosts shop in?
Boo-tiques.

What do you call a person who is broke and stranded in the mall?
Shopwrecked.

• 8 •
MAD MONTHS
AND JOLIDAYS

Why are calendars so popular?
Because they have a date every day of the year.

What is a jelly jar's favorite month?
Jam-uary.

What's a liar's favorite month?
Fib-ruary.

When do soldiers get the most tired?
During the month of March.

When do monkeys fall from the sky?
During Ape-ril showers.

BOOBY TRIPS

Where do loser cowboys go on vacation?
To a dud ranch.

Where do bears go on vacation?
To a hiber-nation.

Where does bacteria go on vacation?
Germany.

Where do dieters go on vacation?
Hungary.

How many peanuts do elephants take on vacation?
As many as they can fit in their trunks.

What do magicians say on Halloween?
   "Trick—or trick?"

What do you call a chubby jack-o'-lantern?
   A plumpkin.

When do turkeys stop eating?
   When they're stuffed.

When do you stuff a rubber turkey?
   On Pranksgiving.

Where do the North Pole elves hang their clothes?
   In the Santa Claus-et (closet).

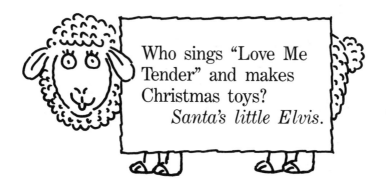

Who sings "Love Me Tender" and makes Christmas toys?
   Santa's little Elvis.

What does Santa have for breakfast?
   Mistletoast.

When does Mrs. Claus mend Santa's socks?
   When they have "ho ho holes".

When does Santa Claus finish delivering his presents?
Just in the St. Nick of time!

In what movie does Santa meet extraterrestrials?
"Claus Encounters."

Why doesn't peanut butter like Christmas?
Because "T'is the season to be jelly. . . ."

What insect doesn't like Christmas?
A bah-humbug.

What is Scrooge's favorite sandwich?
Grueled cheese.

What do you get when your stockings fall off the fireplace, the ornaments drop off the tree, and Santa tracks soot into your living room?
A merry Christmess.

What is Adam's favorite holiday?
New Year's Eve.

What do you get when you eat too much during the holidays?
A Hippy New Year.

• 9 •

WATER WATER EVERYWHERE

Where does water go when it gets ill?
  To the sick bay.

How do you know when a stream needs oil?
  It creeks.

Why did the river go on a diet?
  To take off a few ponds.

What do you get when you cross a body of water and an important nun?
  Lake Superior.

What's the most exact body of water?
The Specific Ocean.

What do you get when you cross the United States and the United Kingdom?
The Atlantic Ocean.

What did the Atlantic Ocean say to the Pacific Ocean?
Nothing, it just waved.

Where does seaweed look for a job?
In the Kelp Wanted ads.

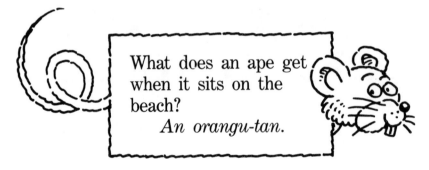

What does an ape get when it sits on the beach?
An orangu-tan.

What city has the most beaches?
Sand Francisco.

What do beaches bet on?
Shore (sure) things.

Where do king crabs live?
In sand castles.

Why couldn't the crab learn to share?
Because it was shellfish.

What kind of lizard loves riddles?
A sillymander.

What do frogs make notes on?
Lily pads.

How do alligators make phone calls?
They croco-dial.

Why couldn't the mermaid go to college?
Because she was a sea ("C") student.

What boats go to college for free?
Scholar ships.

How do you mail a boat?
  You ship it.

What is the world's slowest ship?
  A snailboat.

What do you call an inexperienced rowboat?
  Wet behind the oars (ears).

Where did the boat go when it had a cold?
  To the doc.

Why are docks so unforgiving?
  Because they harbor grudges.

What do you call it when a boat is influenced by other boats at the dock?
  Pier (peer) pressure.

Where does Snow White park her speed-
boat?
At the d'wharf.

What do ravens sail in?
Crowboats.

Why are rowboats such good listeners?
Because they're all oars (ears).

What sizes do flat-bottomed boats come in?
Small, medium and barge.

What do sharks eat with their peanut
butter?
Jellyfish.

What do dolphins do when they fall in love?
They get down on one fin and porpoise (propose).

Where did the fish deposit its allowance?
In the river bank.

How do fish travel up and down in the ocean?
They use an eel-evator.

Where did the octopus enlist?
In the Arms Forces.

Where do you find a down-and-out octopus?
On Squid Row.

What did Jonah say, when asked how he was feeling?
"Very whale, thank you."

What do whales do when they feel sad?
Blubber.

• 10 •

BORED OF EDUCATION

Where did your mother's mother learn the ABC's?

In gramma school.

What do farmers learn in school?

How to tell ripe from wrong.

Where do whistles go to school?

At insti-toots.

Why do thermometers go to school?

To earn their degrees.

ODD AND SUBTRACT

What do you get when you add 1 homework assignment and 1 homework assignment?

2 much homework.

What did the spunky yardstick say to its mother?

"I want to stand on my own three feet."

What practical jokes do mathematicians play?

Arithmetricks.

What do mathematicians use to panel their family rooms?

Multiplywood.

What should you do to help mathematicians with their back problems?

Put them in sub-traction.

Why did the student have to take a class in singing?

Because it was re-choir-ed (required).

How do you know if all the letters of the alphabet are home?
Peek through the K-hole.

Where did cavemen look up synonyms?
In "Roget's Dinosaurus."

What happens when pants cut school?
They get suspendered.

What kind of notebook grows on trees?
Loose leaf.

What fruit studies for exams in a hurry?
Cram-berries.

MATH MYTHS

Who do geometry teachers hang around with?
A small circle of friends.

Why couldn't the geometry teacher walk?
He had a sprained angle.

What kind of math do trees learn?
Twigonometry.

Why don't rabbits carry calculators?
Because they multiply so quickly without them.

Why did the computer have to go to the hospital?
It had a terminal illness.

What did the English teacher say to the class clown?
"Comma down!"

HYSTERICAL HISTORY

How did brave Egyptians write?
In hero-glyphics (hieroglyphics).

Who changed King Tut's diapers?
His mummy.

What did medieval kings ride around their castles in?
Moat-er boats.

What did Sir Lancelot wear to bed?
A knightgown.

What ruler was shorter than Napoleon Bonaparte?
A twelve-inch ruler.

What did King George think of the colonies?
That they were revolting.

Where did Abraham Lincoln keep his pigs?
In a hog cabin.

• 11 •

FUNIDENTIFIED FLYING OBJECTS

How did the radar operator describe the mysterious short-order cook from outer space?
   As an unidentified frying object.

What is the messiest constellation?
   The Big Diaper.

What keeps the sky from falling down?
   Moonbeams.

What is the world's silliest satellite?
A fool (full) moon.

What is the world's craziest satellite?
A moonatic.

What planet is shaped like a fish?
Nep-tuna.

What did the Martian say to the cat?
"Take me to your litter."

How does E.T. read in bed?
He turns on a satellight.

What sports do extraterrestrials play?
Rocket ball.

Why do you need a wrench in the Space Shuttle?
To tighten the astronuts.

Where did the astronaut put his peanut butter sandwich?
In his launch box.

What does a vampire wear to a space shuttle launch?
A Canaveral cape.

What do extraterrestrial lambs travel in?
Spacesheep.

Where do extraterrestrials leave their ships?
At parking meteors.

What poetry do extraterrestrials write?
Uni-verse.

Where do extraterrestrial dentists live?
In the molar system.

What kind of book tells about little green men that don't get along?
Science friction.

• 12 •

OUTRAGEOUS OUTDOORS

What did one tornado say to the other tornado?

"Let's blow this town."

When does rainfall make mistakes?

During a blunderstorm.

What do rich people breathe?

Million-air.

What do you call it when you holler to someone two miles away?

Lung distance.

Why wouldn't the lightning bolt go to the storm?
Because it was on strike.

What swept that repulsive hat off your head?
Dis-gust of wind.

Where do crazy plants grow?
In crackpots.

What do you call blue-colored grass?
Smurf turf.

What do you call a national park that everyone gets lost in?
A bewilderness.

What's the longest rock in the world?
A milestone.

Why was the pile of junk sitting in the middle of the Sahara desert?
For the mirage (garage) sale.

When does Kermit the Frog wake up?
At the croak of dawn.

What is the most modest insect?
The humblebee.

What American grasshopper likes to brave the frontier?
Davy Cricket.

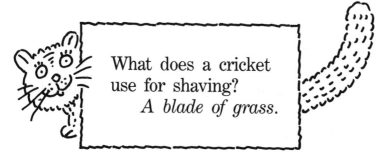

What does a cricket use for shaving?
A blade of grass.

What insects stick around bulletin boards?
Thumb ticks.

What kind of stroller do you wheel an infant insect in?
A baby buggy.

Why was the 2,000-year-old flower wrapped in strips of cloth?
It was a chrysanthemummy.

What did the flower say when it was told to keep a secret?
"Mum's the word!"

What did the tree say when it couldn't solve the riddle?
"I'm stumped."

What young tree always gets taken advantage of?
A sap-ling.

What do you get when you chop down a tuna tree?
Fish sticks.

What happened to her little ones when they disobeyed Mother Earth?
They were grounded.

• 13 •

CRIME AND PUN-ISHMENT

What comic strip superhero drinks apple juice and scales tall buildings?
Ciderman.

Where do you send old detectives?
To the clue factory.

What do you call a low-flying police officer?
A helicopper.

How do police officers patrol the ocean?
In squid cars.

Who is the smallest person on the police force?
The centi-meter maid.

Where do police officers put criminals that steal Hershey's chocolate?
Behind candy bars.

What did one police officer say to the other police officer after the bank was robbed?
"It was all your vault."

What did the police officer say to the tired criminal?
"It looks like you could use a-rrest."

Why did the policeman arrest the letter?
He caught the J walking.

Why did government agents arrest the accountant who wouldn't take a cab?
They got him for taxi evasion.

What did they do to the coffee cup after it was arrested?
Took a mug shot.

What did the prisoner say when he bumped into the governor?
"Pardon me!"

What do you do for a prisoner in a leaking boat?
Bail him out.

Why did the clock strike 12?
Because they struck it first.

How did the jewel thief wake up every morning?
To a burglar alarm.

What do criminals read for fun?
The want-ed ads.

What kind of hives are most dangerous to scratch?
Bee hives.

What color does purple become when it's angry?
Violet (violent).

Why are saddles so hard to get along with?
Because they stirrup trouble.

What do Butch Cassidy and the Sundance Kid roast over an open fire?
Marshal-mallows.

What young outlaw was overweight?
Belly the Kid.

What do you do with the painting of an out-law?

Hang it at sunrise.

What cowboy steals teapots?

A kettle (cattle) rustler.

What crime-fighting gardener rides a horse and wears a mask?

The Lawn Ranger.

What advice did the attorney give to the American Indian?

Sioux (sue).

What did the attorney say to the milk carton?
"I'll see you in quart."

What do nearsighted lawyers wear?

Contract lenses.

What did the president of the Lefties Association say?

"We have rights, too."

What happens to words when they break the law?

They get sentenced.

How did Sir Lancelot settle disagreements?

In knight court.

What did the judge say when the librarian broke the law?

"I'm going to throw the book at you!"

Who cleans up a judge's office?

The chamber maid.

What do you call twelve hurt people who judge guilt and innocence?

An injury.

In what state are the most secrets uncovered?

South Decoder.

What do secret agents invest their money in?

James Bonds.

What do hangmen read?

"The Daily Noose."

• 14 •

HAPPILY EVER LAUGHTER

Where does Mother Goose leave her garbage?

At the Humpty Dump.

What did the gingerbread man's grandfather use for walking?

A candy cane.

What does Mickey Mouse's girlfriend wear?

Minnie (mini) skirts.

What singing grasshopper lives in a fire-place?

Chimney Cricket.

What man slept in his clothes for 100 years?

Rip Van Wrinkled.

What is the name of the story about the athlete and the giant?

"Jock and the Beanstalk."

What does Jack's giant do when he plays football?

He fee-fi-fo-fumbles.

What lamb stuck itself with a spindle and fell asleep for 100 years?

Sheeping Beauty.

What does Sleeping Beauty gargle with?
   Rinse Charming.

What brand of toilet paper does Sleeping Beauty use?
   Prince Charmin.

Where do stupid princes come from?
   Kingdum-dums.

What happens to stupid princes?
   They get throne out (thrown out).

What powerful reptile lives in Emerald City?
   The Lizard of Oz.

What heavy snowstorm covered Emerald City?
   The Blizzard of Oz.

What nursery rhyme chicken lost her sheep?
   Little Bo Peep-Peep.

What happened to Little Bo Peep after she spent all day looking for her sheep?
   She was Little Bo Pooped.

Who helped Cinderella's cat go to the ball?
Its furry godmother.

What sign did the real estate agent put in front of the Old Woman Who Lived in a Shoe's house?
"Soled."

What dancer spins straw into gold?
Rhumba-stiltskin.

What do short fairy tale characters wear to look taller?
Rumple-stilts.

Who do mice see when they get sick?
The Hickory Dickory Doc.

What did Ali Baba write on?
Sandpaper.

What legendary character steals from the rich and keeps it?
Robin Hoodlum.

• 15 •

DRIVE YOURSELF CRAZY!

What do you call a brainy locomotive?
A train of thought.

What locomotive wears sneakers?
A shoe-shoe train.

What do you get if you cross a happy puppy with a locomotive?
Waggin' train.

How can you tell if a train is happy?
It whistles while it works.

What state has the
most trains?
Massachoochoo.

How does a train blow bubbles?
With choo-chooing gum.

When time flies, where does the pilot sit?
In the clockpit.

What kind of flying lessons are best to avoid?
Crash courses.

What sea creature is found in every car?
A steering whale.

WHEELY FUNNY

What car runs on electricity?
A Voltswagen.

What car can't stop crying?
A Saab (sob).

What's the world's meanest car?
Attila the Hyundai (Hun).

What car can leap tall buildings in a single bound?
A Super-u (Subaru).

What family car doesn't move?
A stationary wagon.

What is a chauffeur's favorite drink?
Limo-nade.

Where shouldn't you ever park a protein?
In front of a carbohydrant.

MECHANIC PANIC

Why did the tailpipe see the mechanic?
It was exhausted.

Why did the car radio see the mechanic?
For a tune-up.

Why did the mechanic call the exterminator?
To get the bugs out of the engine.

Where do mechanics wear earrings?
On their ear lubes (lobes).

What does a car mechanic do when he's 65?
He re-tires.

Why was the silly gasoline pump embarrassed?
Because it made a fuel of itself.

TICKLISH TICKETS

Why did the sheep get a ticket?
For making a ewe (U) turn.

Why did the farmer get a ticket?
He exceeded the seed limit.

Why did the swimmer get a ticket?
He was caught diving without a license.

Why did the pilot get a ticket?
For going the wrong way on a runway (one way) street.

Where do automobiles do the backstroke?
In car pools.

What do you call it when a car hits a candy machine?
A vender bender.

What do cars eat from?
License plates.

What kind of book did Chitty Chitty Bang Bang write about itself?
An auto–biography.

Was the blimp crazy?
Yes, it was a balloonatic.

What do you get when a bike freezes?
An ice-cycle (icicle).

Why couldn't the little boy see his bicycle after he parked it behind a tree?
Because the bark was bigger than his bike.

• 16 •
PARTY LINES

What do little potatoes play on in the park?
A tater-totter (teeter-totter).

What did King Kong play on in the park?
The monkey bars.

Where do small camels play?
In sandboxes.

What does a baby snake play with?
A rattle.

What do Japanese children play with?
Tokyo-yos.

What do you call a fun-loving toddler that wears diapers?
A potty (party) animal.

When do candles party?
On wickends.

Where do pickles party?
In a barrel of fun.

What is the worst flower to invite to a party?
A daffo-dull.

What is the worst musical instrument to play at your party?
A humdrum.

What do you call a musician who pretends he can play the sax?
A saxophone-y.

What music do steel workers play at their parties?
Heavy metal.

What state loves Latino music?
Ala-bamba.

How can you find out how many vampires attended the party?
Just count Dracula.

What state has the loudest parties?
Illinoise.

What do monsters use to decorate parties?
Creep (crepe) paper.

COOK OUT BELOW!

Where does a Ken doll grill his hamburgers?
On a Barbie-cue.

Where do monkeys barbecue their hamburgers?
On grillas.

What do cannibals barbecue?
Speared (spare) ribs.

NAME THAT GAME

What is a mouse's favorite game?
Hide 'n squeak.

What is a faucet's favorite game?
Hide 'n leak.

What is a parrot's favorite game?
Hide 'n speak.

What is a thief's favorite game?
Hide 'n sneak.

What is a surfer's favorite game?
Tide 'n seek.

What is a sled's favorite game?
Glide 'n seek.

What is the playground's favorite game?
Slide 'n seek.

NAME THAT GAME

What is Dr. Pepper's favorite game?
Follow the Liter.

What is a whale's favorite game?
Swallow the Leader.

What is a fish's favorite game?
Salmon Says.

What is a priest's favorite game?
Ring around the Rosary.

What is a quarterback's favorite game?
Tick-Tackle-Toe.

What is Big Foot's favorite game?
Tick-Tack-Toes.

What do mermaids eat at birthday parties?
Fishcakes.

What do cannibals eat at parties?
Lady fingers.

What musical group performs at marriage ceremonies?

A wedding band.

Where does a computer go to dance?

To a disk-o.

What is a fish's favorite dance step?

The fox-trout (fox trot).

What did Fred Astaire and Ginger Rogers put on the floor of their dance studio?

Waltz-to-waltz carpeting.

What did one perfume say to the other perfume?

"Cologne at last."

What do you say when the Long Ranger wears cologne?

"Who was that musked man?"

• 17 •

FUNNY BUSINESS

What pen company is in business one day and out of business the next?
Disappearing Inc. (Ink).

When can one man be more than one man?
When he's Foreman.

What do plumbers smoke?
Pipes.

What vegetables can predict the future?
   E. S. Peas.

How do hypnotists get around without a car?
   They use public trance-portation.

Where do old ministers go?
   Out to pastor (pasture).

Why did the wacky farmer hire a maid?
   To dust his crops.

What did the wacky carpenter do before he went to bed each night?
   He made his bed.

What computer course do beginning pro-
grammers take when they join the army?
Basic training.

What 20 lb. bag of dry food do 30-year-old
executives buy?
Yuppie Chow.

What do attorneys wear to work?
Lawsuits.

What do attorneys wear under their suits?
Briefs.

What did one dollar say to the other dollar?
"I want to be a loan (alone)."

What do you get when you cross ten million
dollars and bank employees?
Fortune tellers.

What do fortune tellers plant around the
house?
Palm trees.

How do fortune tellers predict future sales?
They look in their crystal malls.

What do psychics get when they go to the
doctor?
A meta-physical.

What kind of award do you give a dentist?
A plaque.

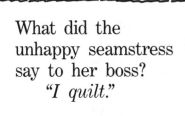

What did the
unhappy seamstress
say to her boss?
"I quilt."

What does an unhappy tailor do to wrinkled pants?
He de-presses them.

What did the tailor say when asked how he was feeling?
"Sew-sew."

Why was Sir Lancelot always so tired?
Because he worked the knight shift.

How do doctors prescribe sleeping pills?
In small dozes.

Why did the doctor operate on the book?
He wanted to remove its appendix.

What medical problems do many painters have?
Art (heart) attacks.

Why did the paintbrush retire?
It had a stroke.

How does an artist break up with his girlfriend?
He gives her the brush-off.

What famous nurse never had time to get dressed in the morning?
Florence Nightingown.

Why did the dogcatcher catch so many large dogs?
Because he was getting paid by the pound.

What do you call a messy mailman?
A litter carrier.

Where can you find an unconscious barber?
In a comb-a.

What do you say to a barber when you want
him to cut your hair faster?
"Make it snippy!"

Why did the barber win the race?
He knew a short cut.

Where do barbers keep their money?
In shavings banks.

What do basketmakers do when it's time to
go?
Weave goodbye!

Index

Accountant, 67
Actor, 9
Adam, 46
Agents, secret, 70
Ali Baba, 74
Alligators, 49
Alphabet, 55
Animals, 19-24
Ape, 9, 48
Astaire, Fred, 86
Astronauts, 60
Athlete, 35, 72
Attorney, 69, 89
Auctions, 41
Australians, 19
Autobiography, 76

Babar, 7
Babe Ruth, 36
Baby, 32
Bacteria, 44
Ball, 73
Ballerina, 12
Band leader, 11
Banks, 92
Barbecue, 83
Barber, 6, 11, 92
Baseball, 36
Basement, 26
Basketmakers, 92
Bathroom, 37
Beach, 48
Bears, 8, 21, 44
Beatles, 17
Bee, 11, 63, 68
Bicycle, 16, 80
Big Foot, 16, 85
Big Mac, 31
Bird, 17
Blimps, 25, 80
Bloomingdales, 40
Boats, 49, 50, 51, 57, 67
Body-builders, 35
Bogart, Humphrey, 8
Bonaparte, Napoleon, 57
Bond, James, 70
Book, 34, 48
Bowling, 37
Breakfast, 16, 29-30, 45
Bricklayers, 28
Brontosaurus, 20, 35
Bulletin boards, 63

Bullfighter, 33
Butter, 30

Calculators, 56
Calendars, 43
Camels, 81
Candles, 82
Candy, 66; machine, 79
Cane, candy, 71
Cannibals, 83, 85
Carbohydrates, 77
Card game, 38
Carpenter, 88
Carpet, 37
Cars, 8, 77-79
Cartoons, 8
Casper the Friendly Ghost, 13
Cassidy, Butch, 68
Cats, 22, 59, 73; wild, 6, 30
Cavemen, 55
Cereal, 10, 29
Chain, 39
Chair, 26
Chauffeur, 77
Cheers, 38
Cheese, 31
Chef, 30, 33, 34
Chess, 30
Chicken, 73
Chimney, 27
Chipmunk, 7
Chitty Chitty Bang Bang, 76
Christmas, 45-46
Church, 15
Cinderella, 73
Clock, 67
Clothes, 40
Coffee mug, 67
College, 49
Comedy, 12
Comics, 12
Commercial, 42
Computer, 31, 56, 86; course, 89
Con man, 37
Cookie, 6
Couch, 28
Cowboy, 9, 34, 44, 69
Cows, 24
Crabs, 48, 49
Cricket, 63
Criminals, 65-69

Dance, 17
Dancer, 74
Dancing, 86
Deer, 20
Dentists, 60, 91
Dessert, 22, 33
Detectives, 65
Devito, Danny, 6
Dictionary, 16, 20
Diet, 47
Dieters, 44
Dinner, 22
Dinosaurs, 20, 35
Disc jockeys, 6
Doctor, 89; foot, 33
Dogs, 11, 23, 90
Dollar, 89
Dolphins, 6, 52
Door, 25, 26
Dracula, 18, 83
Drink, 22, 77
Duck, 23
Dumbo, 19

Earrings, 78
Eggs, 12
Egyptians, 57
Electric company, 28
Elephant, 19, 44
Elevator, 13
Elves, 45
Emerald City, 73
Empire State Building, 33
ESP, 88
E.T., 59
Exams, 56
Exterminator, 78
Extraterrestrials, 59

Farmers, 36, 53, 79, 88
Faucet, 84
Fighters, 36
Firefighters, 41
Fireplace, 72
Fish, 8, 11, 52, 59, 86; sticks, 64
Flintstone, Fred, 8
Flowers, 40, 63, 64, 82
Flu, 27
Flying, 80
Food, 22, 29-34, 83
Football, 72, 85; team, 38
Fortune tellers, 89
Frankenstein, 14
Freud, Sigmund, 31
Frogs, 49

Fruit, 56
Furniture, 27

Game, 17, 40, 84, 85; shows, 5, 6
Garage sale, 63
Gardener, 69
Gasoline pump, 78
Genie, 18
Geometry, 56
George, King, 57
Germany, 44
Ghost, 13, 16, 42
Giant, 72
Gingerbread man, 34, 71
Giraffes, 21
Gnomes, 18
Golf, 37, 38
Goose, Mother, 71
Grass, 22, 62
Grasshopper, 63, 72
Guitar, 10
Gum, 32, 76
Gunfighter, 6

Hair, 21
Hamburgers, 33, 83
Hangman, 70
Hat, 62
History, 57
Hives, 68
Hockey players, 12
Horses, 6, 8, 18, 24
Hospital, 56
House, 25-28
Humpty Dumpty, 71
Hungary, 44
Hypnotist, 88
Hyundai, 77

Ice, 15
Ice cream, 33
Idea, 26
Igor the Hunchback, 18
Indian, American, 26, 64
Insect, 46, 63

Jack-o'-lantern, 45
Jedi, 9
Jewel thief, 67
Jock, 72; see Athlete
Jockeys, 37
Jokes, 10, 12, 38; practical, 54
Jonah, 52
Judge, 70
Jury, 70

Kangaroos, 19, 20
Kent, Clark, 33
Kermit the Frog, 63
King Kong, 15, 81
Knight, 33, 57, 90; court, 70;
    Gladys, 38
Knives, 41

Lambs, 60, 72
Lancelot, Sir, 57, 70, 90
Laundromat, 18
Lawyers, 69
Lefties Association, 69
Lemon, 41
Letter, 21
Liars, 41, 43
Librarian, 70
Light bulb, 28
Lightning, 62
Lincoln, Abraham, 36, 57
Little Bo Peep, 73
Lizards, 27, 49, 73
Locomotives, 75
Lone Ranger, 33, 86
Lunch, 22, 30

Magicians, 45
Mailman, 91
Mall, 39, 41, 42, 89
Marriage, 15, 21, 22, 83
Martian, 59
Math, 54, 56
Mechanic, car, 78
Mermaid, 49, 85
Mice, 74
Millionaire, 11, 30, 61
Ministers, 88
Monkeys, 44
Monster, 5, 13-18, 83
Months, 43, 44
Moon, 59
Moose, 20
Mother Earth, 64
Mouse, 84; Mickey, 71
Movie, 9, 14, 46
Mummy, 57
Muppets, 6
Music, 10, 11, 82-83
Musical, 11; instrument, 10

National park, 62
New Year, 46
Niagara Falls, 22
Noise, 32, 83
Nun, 47

Nurse, 91
Nursery rhyme characters, 71-74

Occupations, 87-95
Oceans, 48
Octopus, 52
Opera, 7
Orchestra, 11
Outer space, 58-60
Outfielder, 11
Outlaw, 68, 69
Oz, 73

Painters, 25, 90, 91
Palmer, Arnold, 38
Pancakes, 30
Parasols, 41
Parrot, 84
Parties, 82-85
Pasta, 7, 33
Pen company, 87
Pepper, Dr., 85
Perfume, 86
Phone, 27
Photographers, 14
Piano, 15
Pickles, 82
Pig, 30, 36
Pillsbury Doughboy, 34
Pilot, 79, 80
Planet, 59
Plants, 62
Playground, 84
Plumber, 37, 87
Poetry, 60
Polar bears, 21
Police, 65, 66
Porch, 26
Potato, 81
Priest, 85
Princes, 73
Prisoner, 67
Prize fighter, 36
Protein, 77
Psychics, 89
Punch, fruit, 7
Puppet, 6
Puppy, 75

Quilt, 90

Rabbit, 22, 56
Race, 92
Radio, car, 78
Rainfall, 61

Ravens, 51
Real estate agent, 74
Retirement, 78
Rip Van Wrinkle, 72
River, 47
Robin Hood, 74
Rock, 63
Rogers, Ginger, 86
Rooster, 23
Ruler, 57
Rumplestiltskin, 74

Saab, 77
Saddles, 68
Sahara desert, 63
Sailing, 18
Sailors, 42
Salmon, 8, 85
Sandpaper, 74
Santa Claus, 45, 46
Satellite, 59
Scarecrows, 31
School, 16, 38, 53-58
Science fiction, 60
Seal, 26
Seamstress, 90
Seaweed, 48
Secret, 64, 70
Sharks, 51
Sheep, 24, 28, 38, 60, 73, 79
Shopping, 39-42
Siamese twins, 28
Singing, 8, 54
Sled, 84
Sleeping Beauty, 72, 73
Smokey the Bear, 30
Snack, 31
Snake, 81
Sneakers, 75
Snoopy, 31
Snow White, 51
Soldiers, 44
Song, 17
Space, 60
Spaghetti, 32, 33
Sports, 35-39, 59
Star Wars, 9
State, 76, 82, 83
Stores, 40; see Shopping
Storm, 10, 62
Stove, 27
Subaru, 77

Sundance Kid, 68
Sunshine, 21
Superhero, 65
Superior, Lake, 47
Supermarket, 39
Surfer, 84
Surgeon, 6
Swimmers, 30, 79
Synonyms, 55

Table, 26
Tailor, 90
Tailpipe, 78
Talk shows, 5
Taxi, 67
Tea, 15, 22
Telephones, 37, 41
Thermometers, 53
Thief, 67, 84
Tickets, 79
Ticks, 63
Toast, 30
Toilet paper, 73
Tornado, 61
Track and field, 36
Traffic, 20
Train, 75, 76; engineer, 36
Trees, 5, 55, 56, 64
Turkeys, 22, 45
TV, 5-6

Umpire, 9, 36

Vacations, 44
Vampires, 60, 83; see Dracula
Vegetables, 88
Volkswagen, 77

Water, 47-52
Weather, 37, 61; man, 10
Werewolf, 13
Whale, 12, 52, 76, 85
Whistles, 53
Wind, 62
Window, 26
Witch, 16-18; doctor, 15
Wizards, 15
Words, 69
Worms, 32
Wright brothers, 42

Yogi Bear, 8
Yoyos, 82
Yuppies, 89